Fashion & Portrait Coloring Book for Grown-Ups

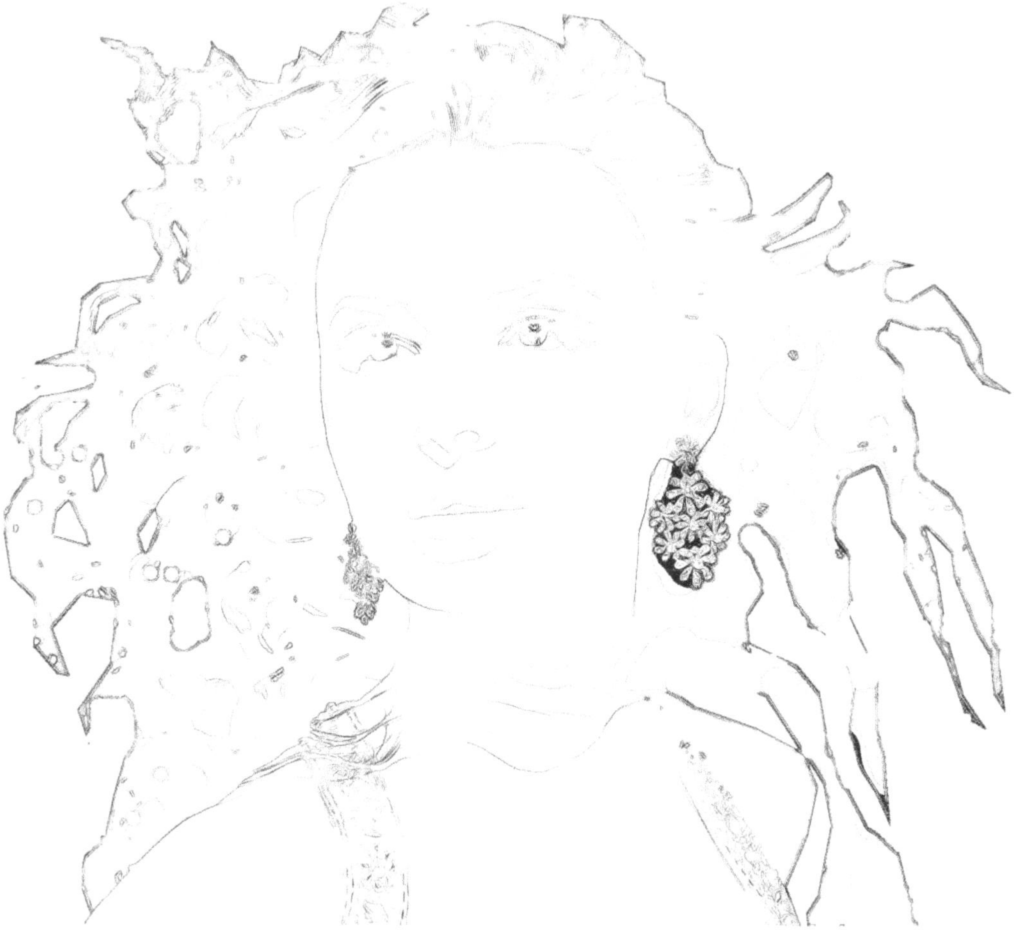

Anthony Hutzler

Sketch Coloring Book

Copyright: Published in the United States by Anthony Hutzler
Published July 2016

All rights reserved. No part of this publication may be reproduced, stored in retrieval system, copied in any form or by any means, electronic, mechanical, photocopying, recording or otherwise transmitted without written permission from the publisher. Please do not participate in or encourage piracy of this material in any way. You must not circulate this book in any format. Anthony Hutzler does not control or direct users' actions and is not responsible for the information or content shared, harm and/or actions of th

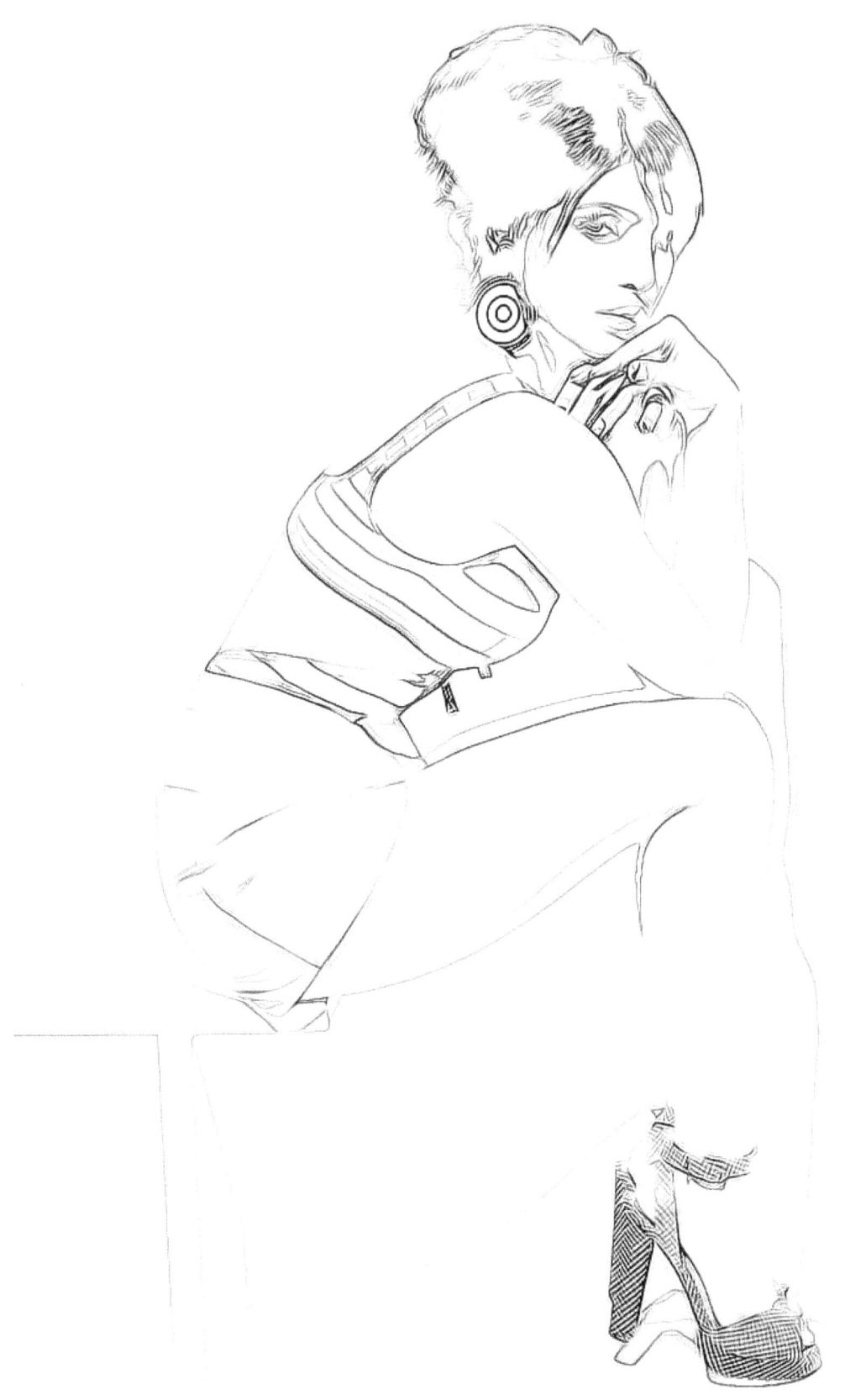

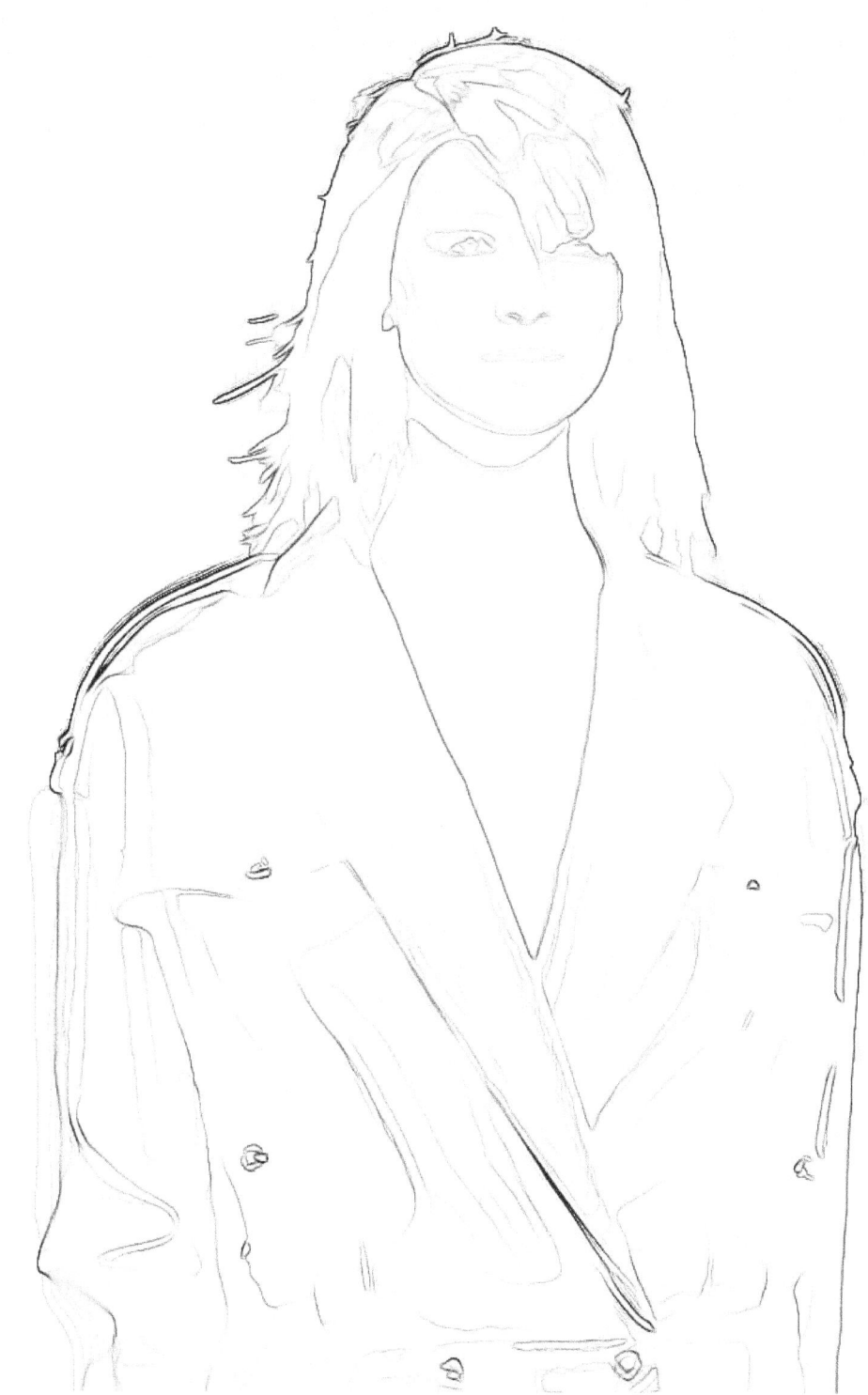

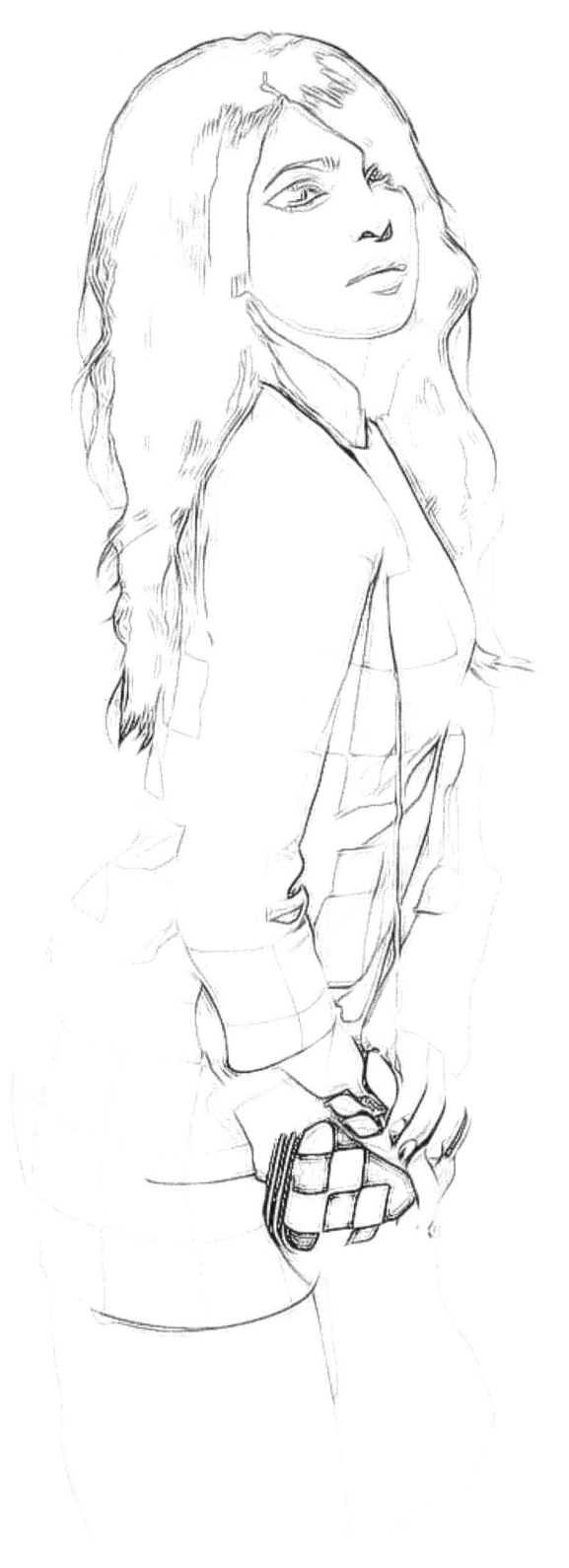

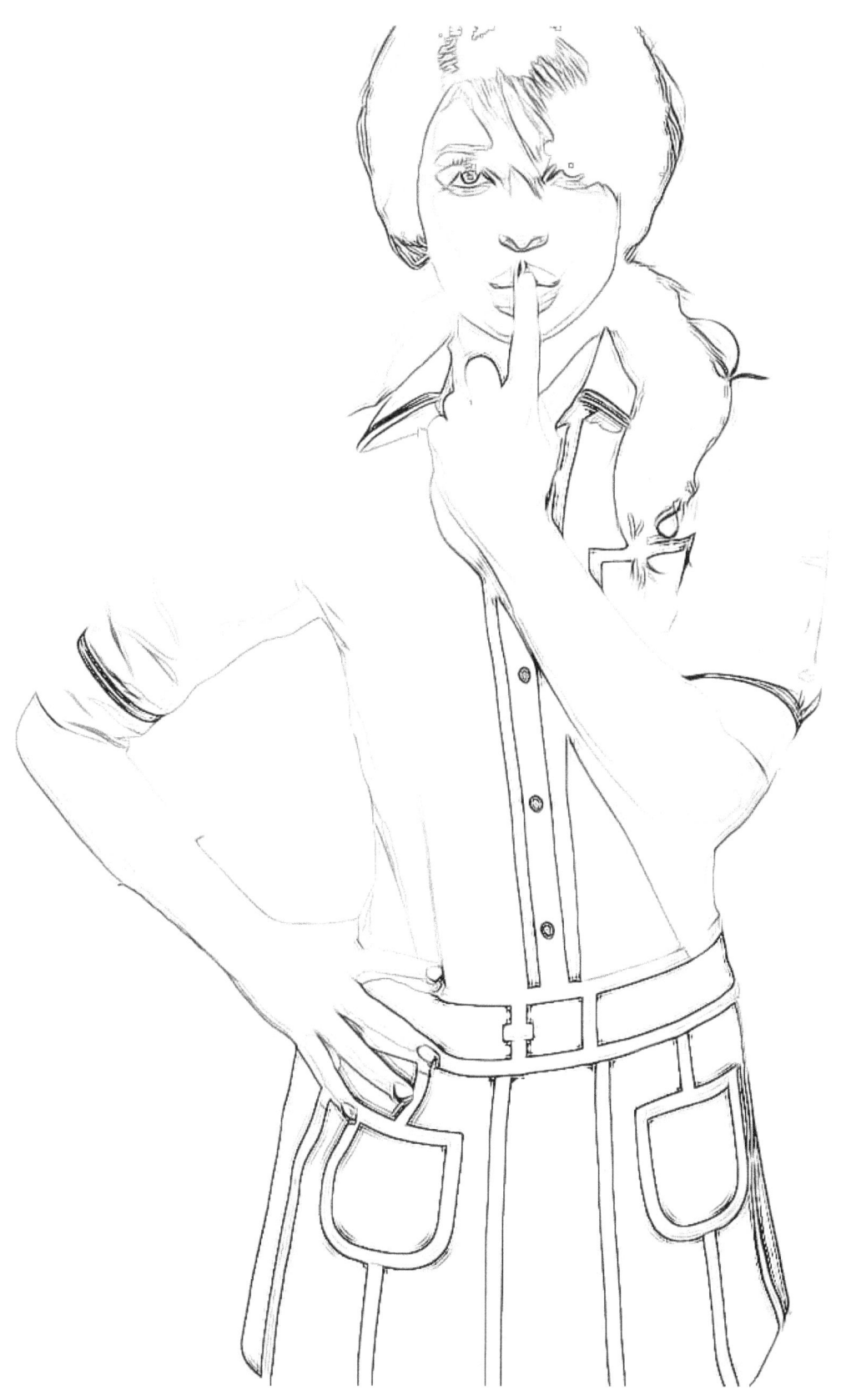

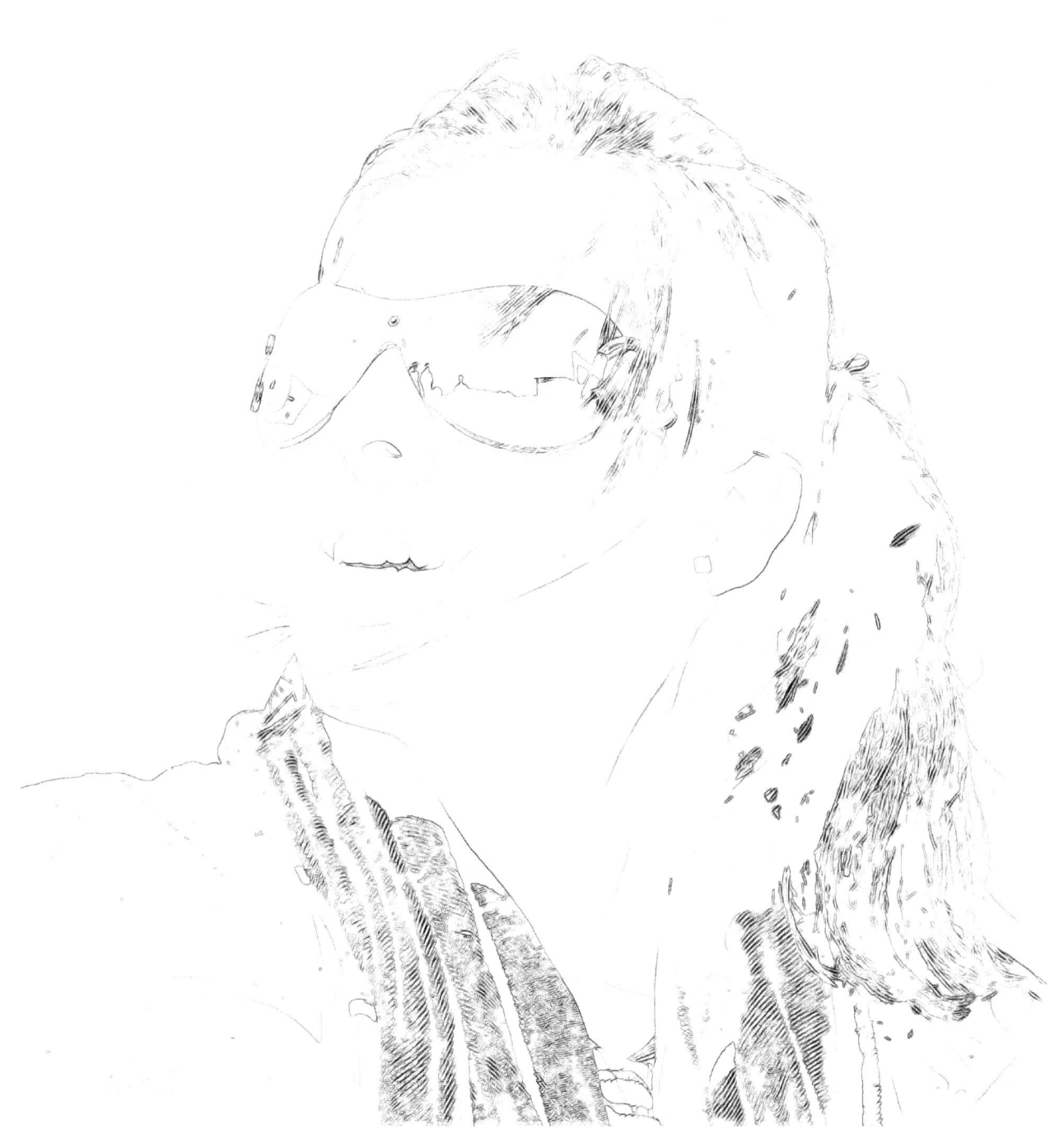

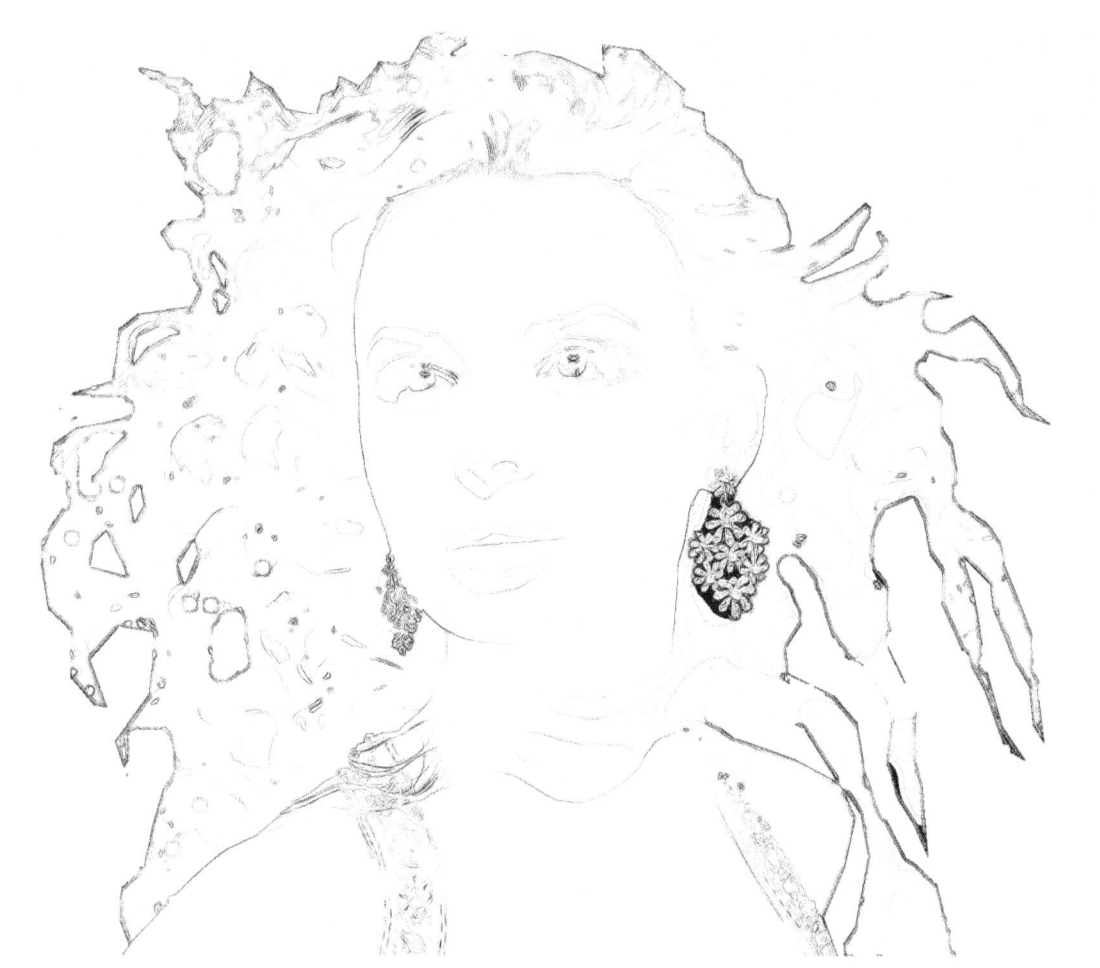

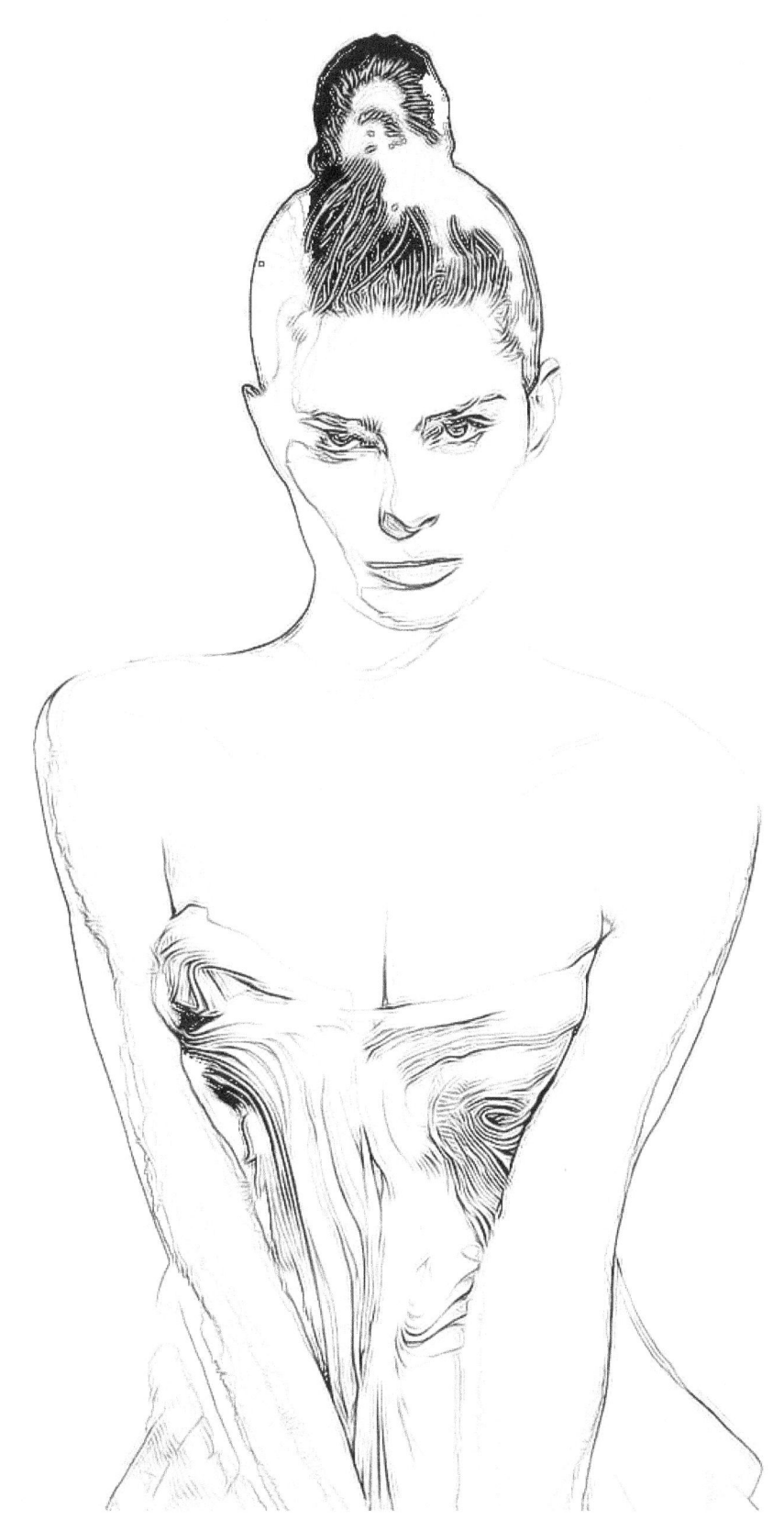

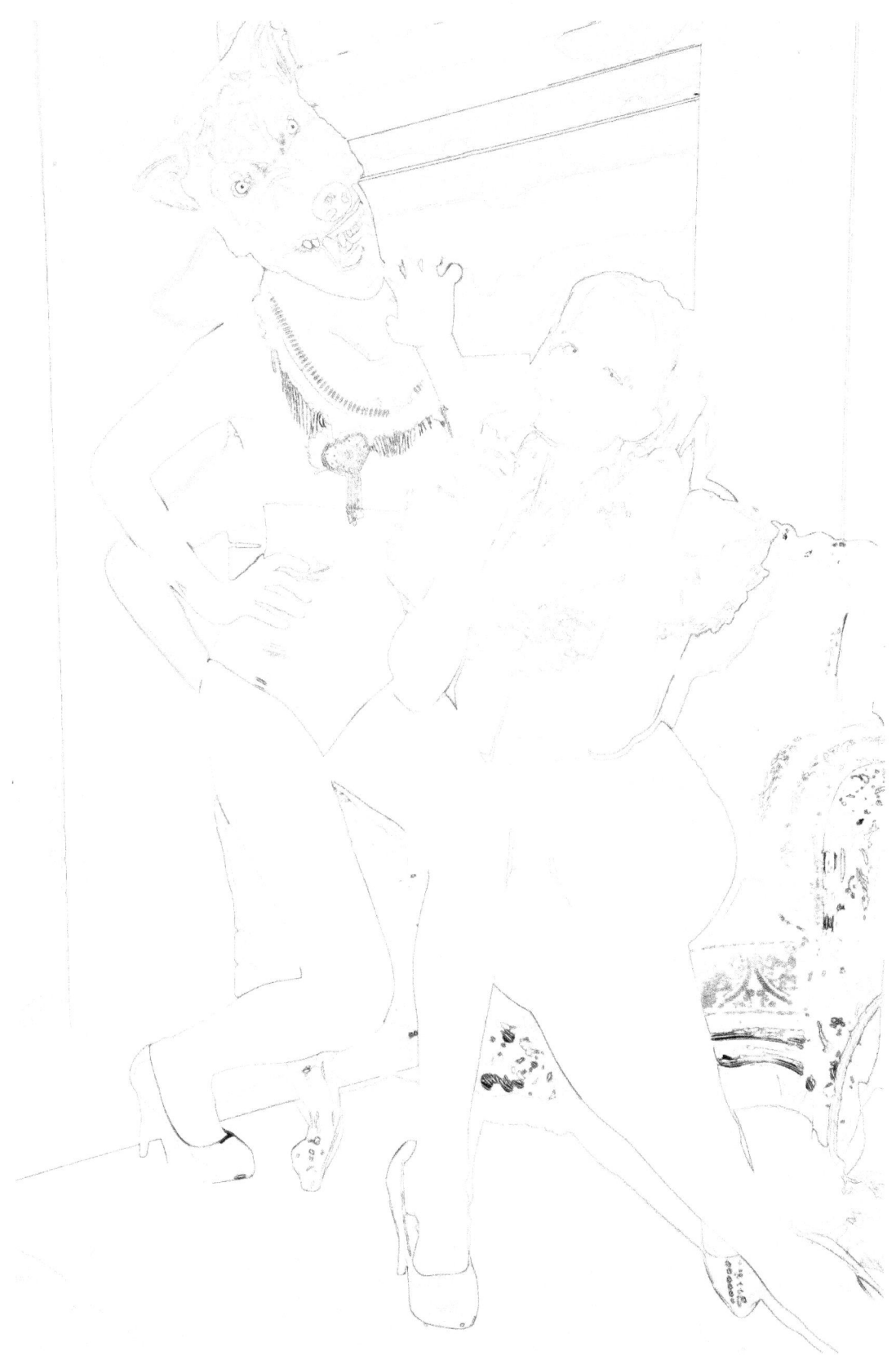

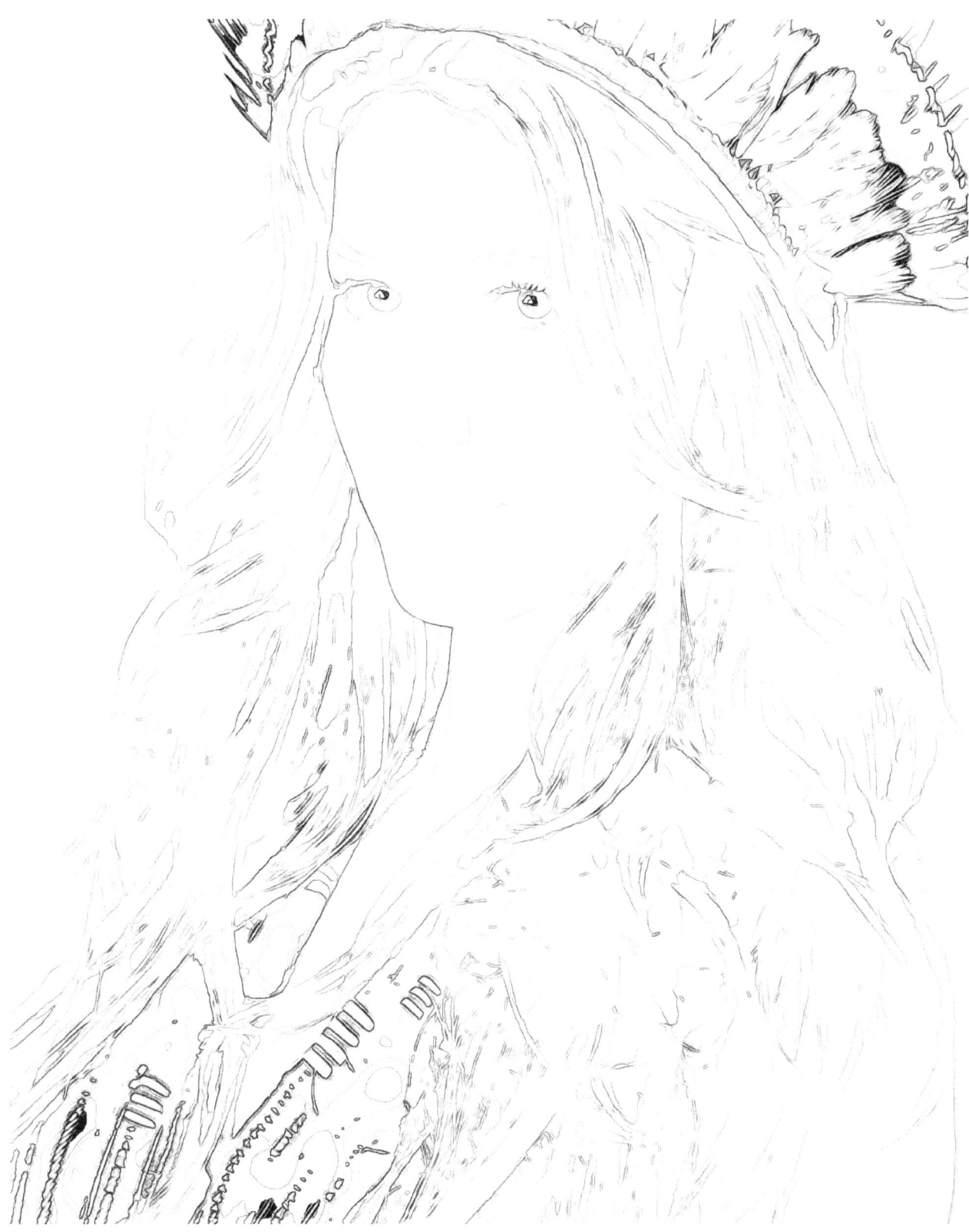

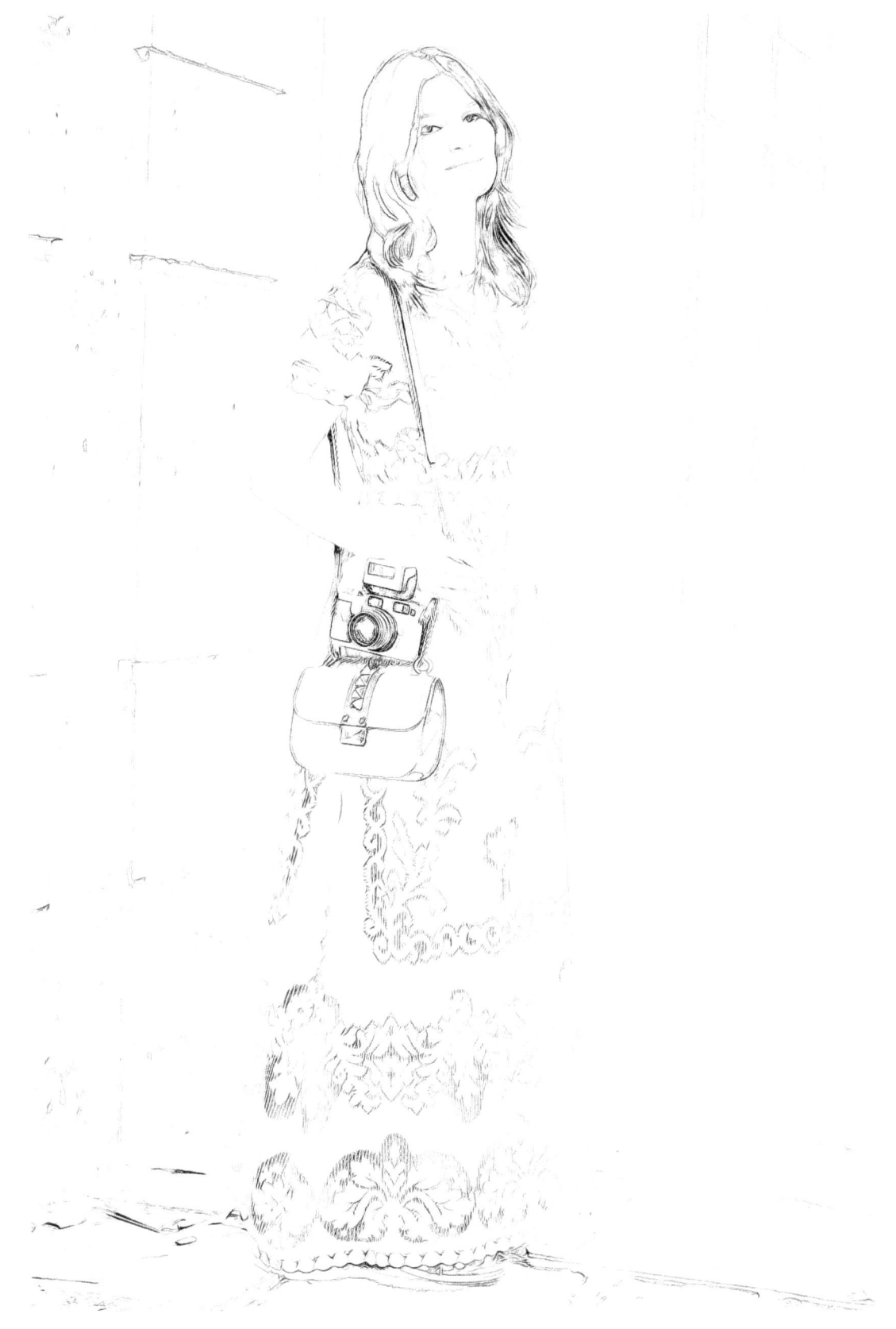

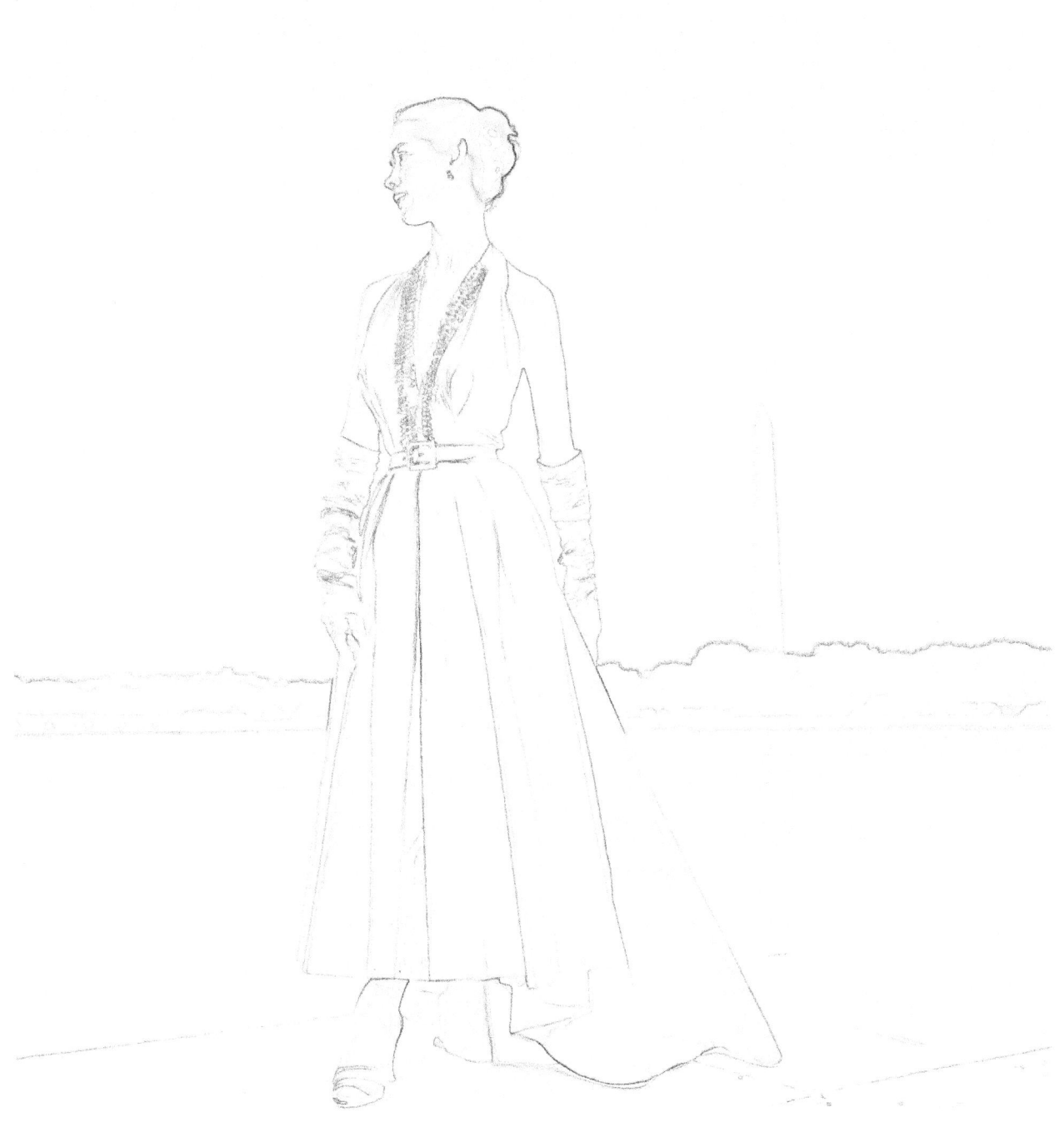

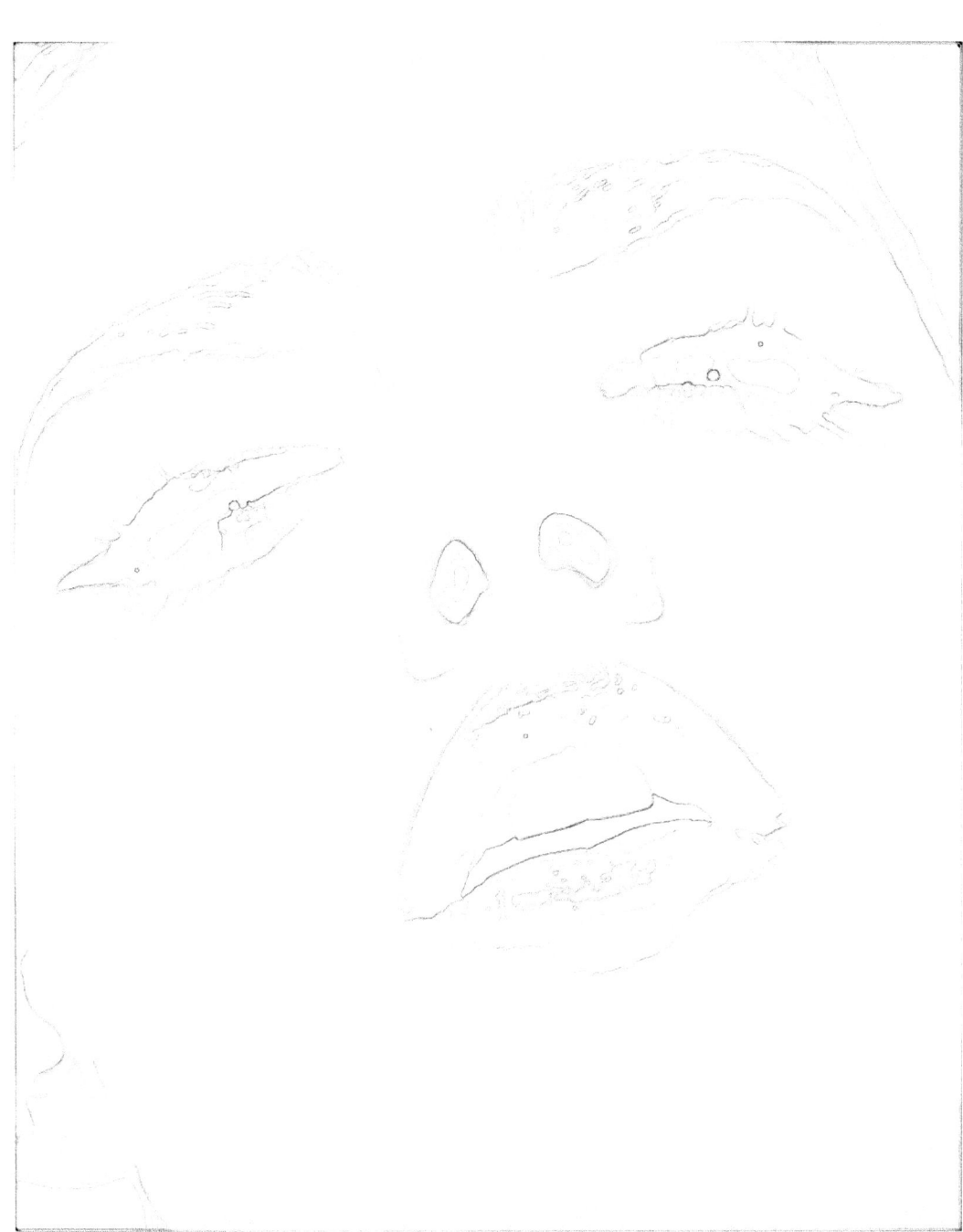

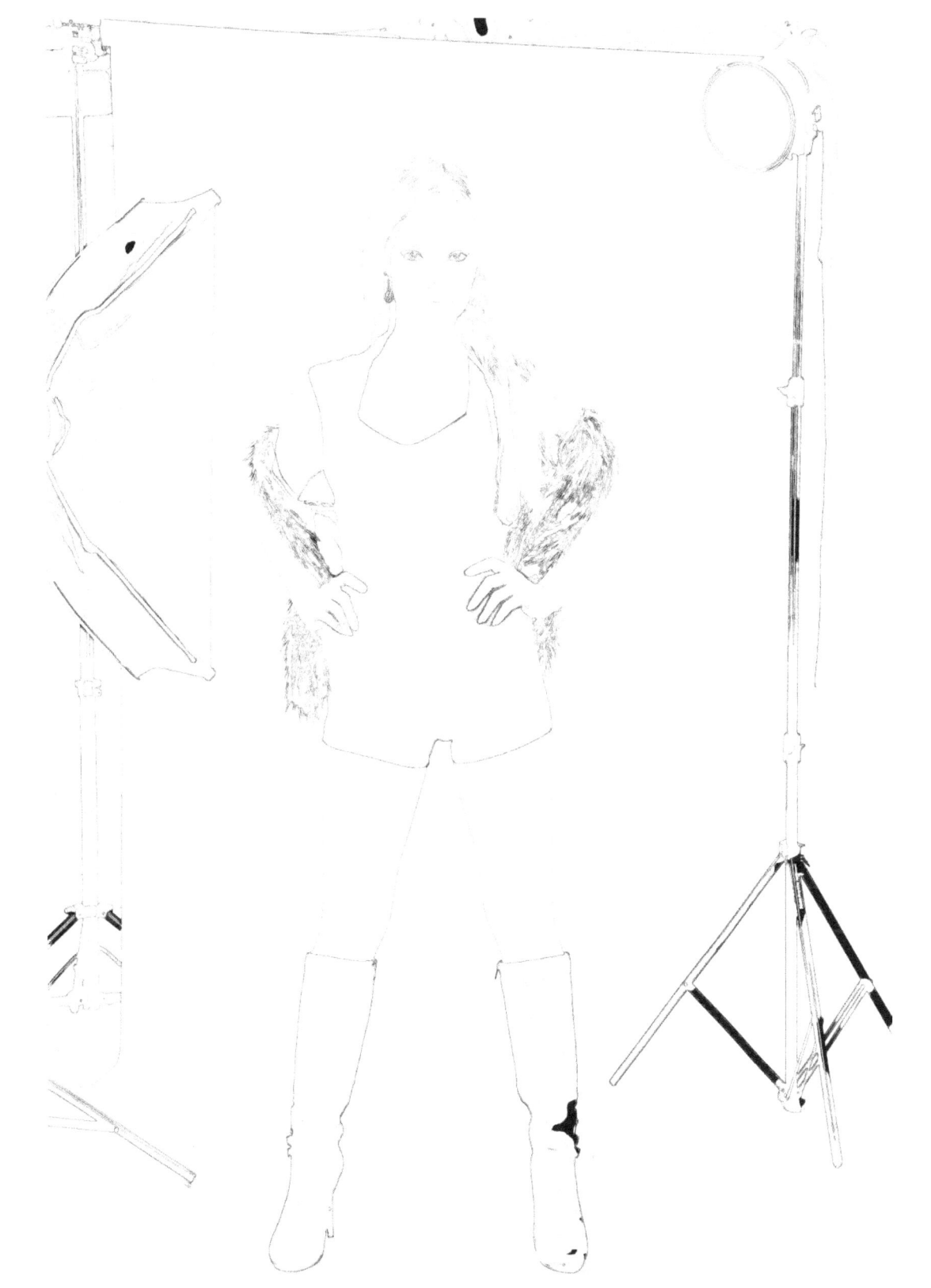

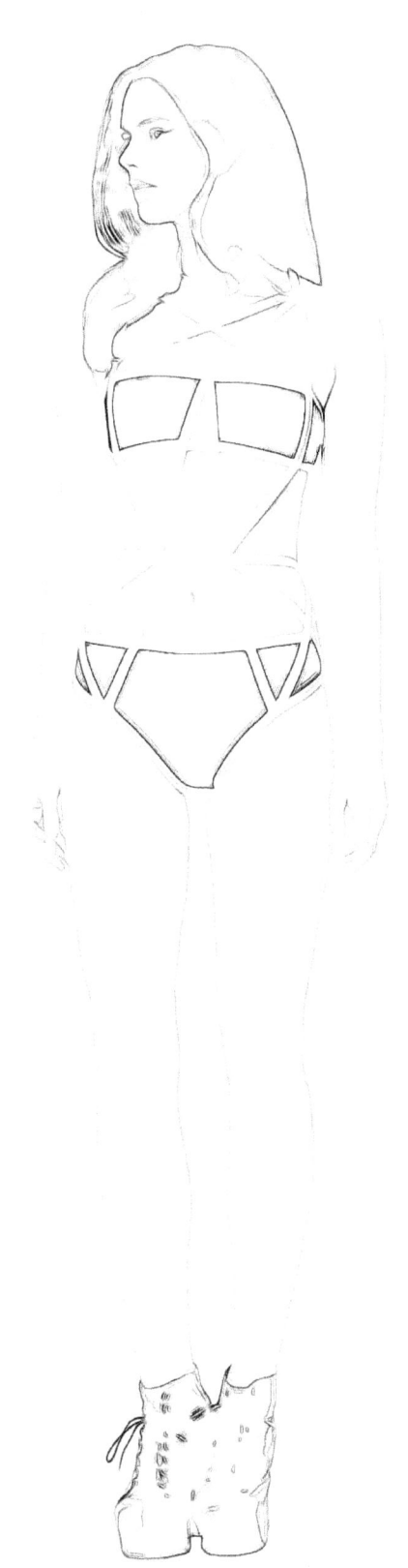

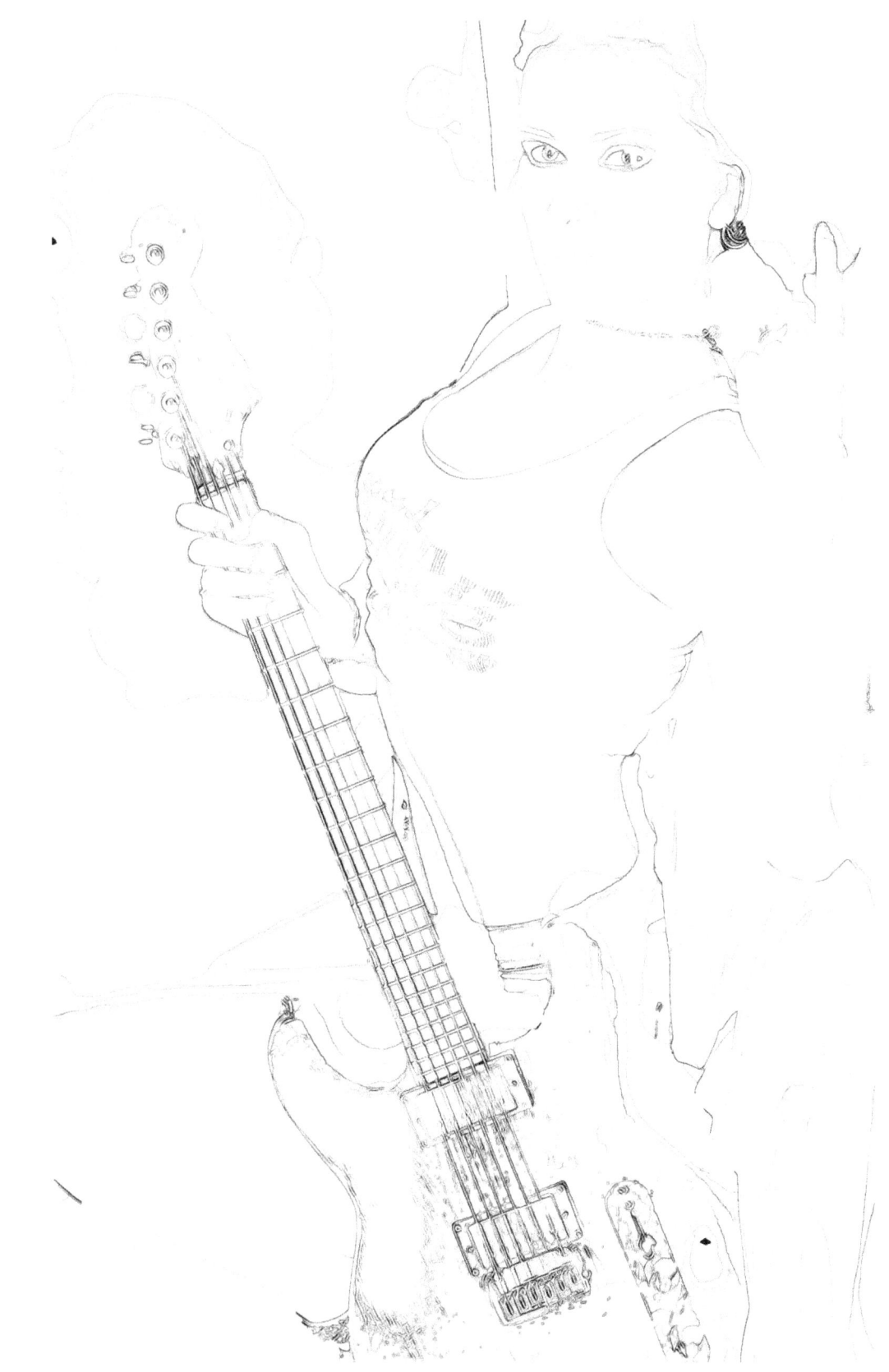

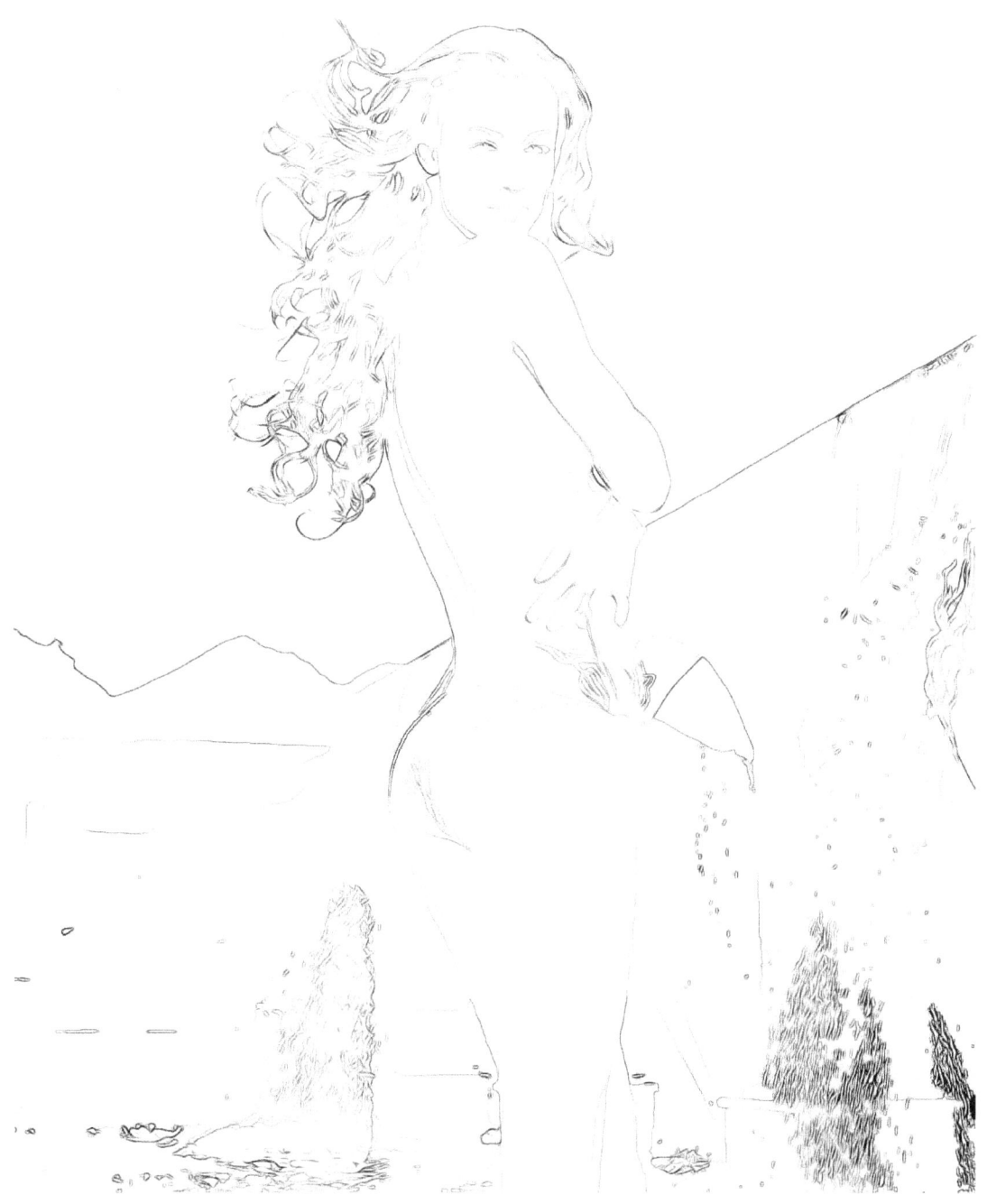

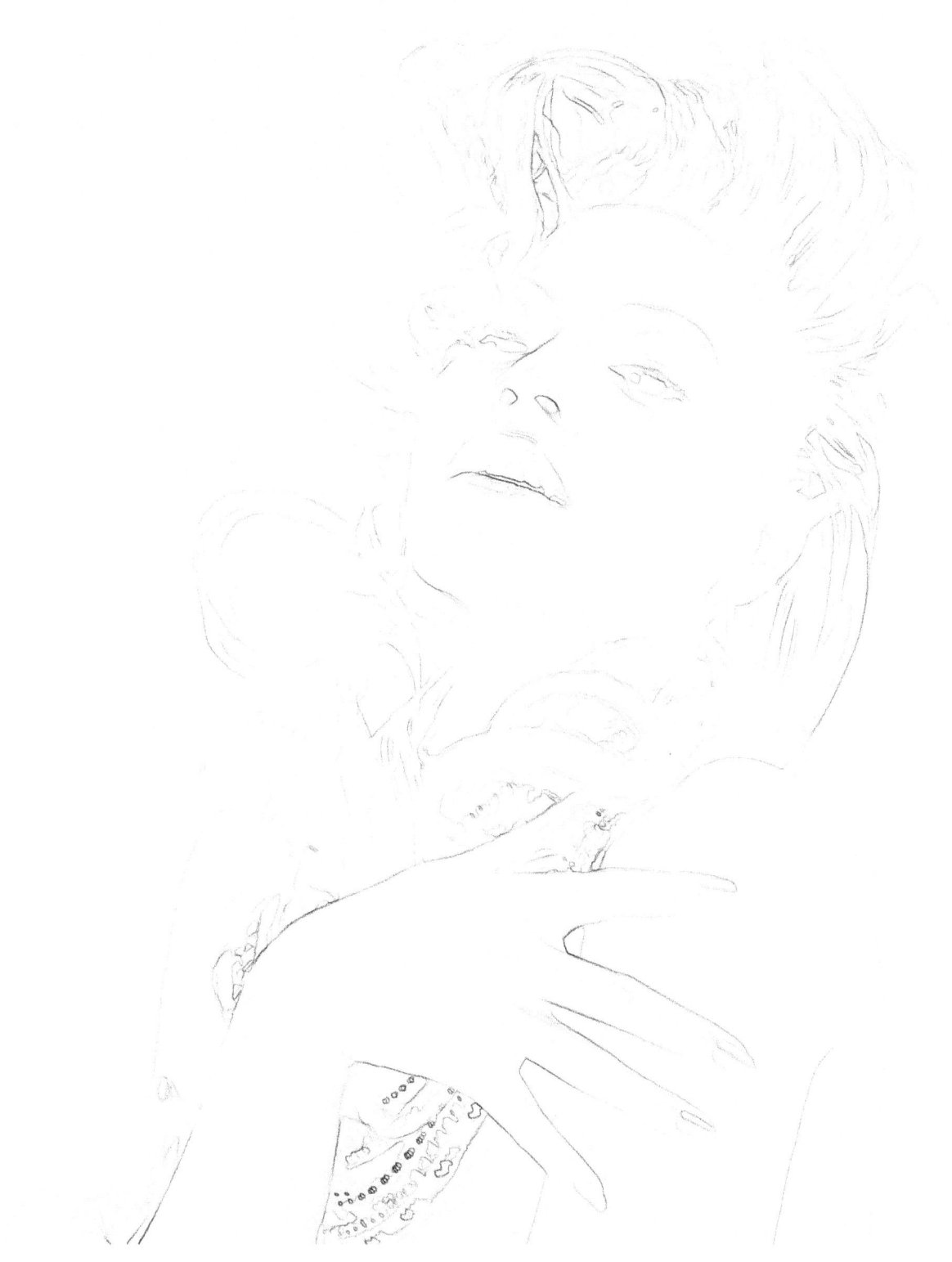

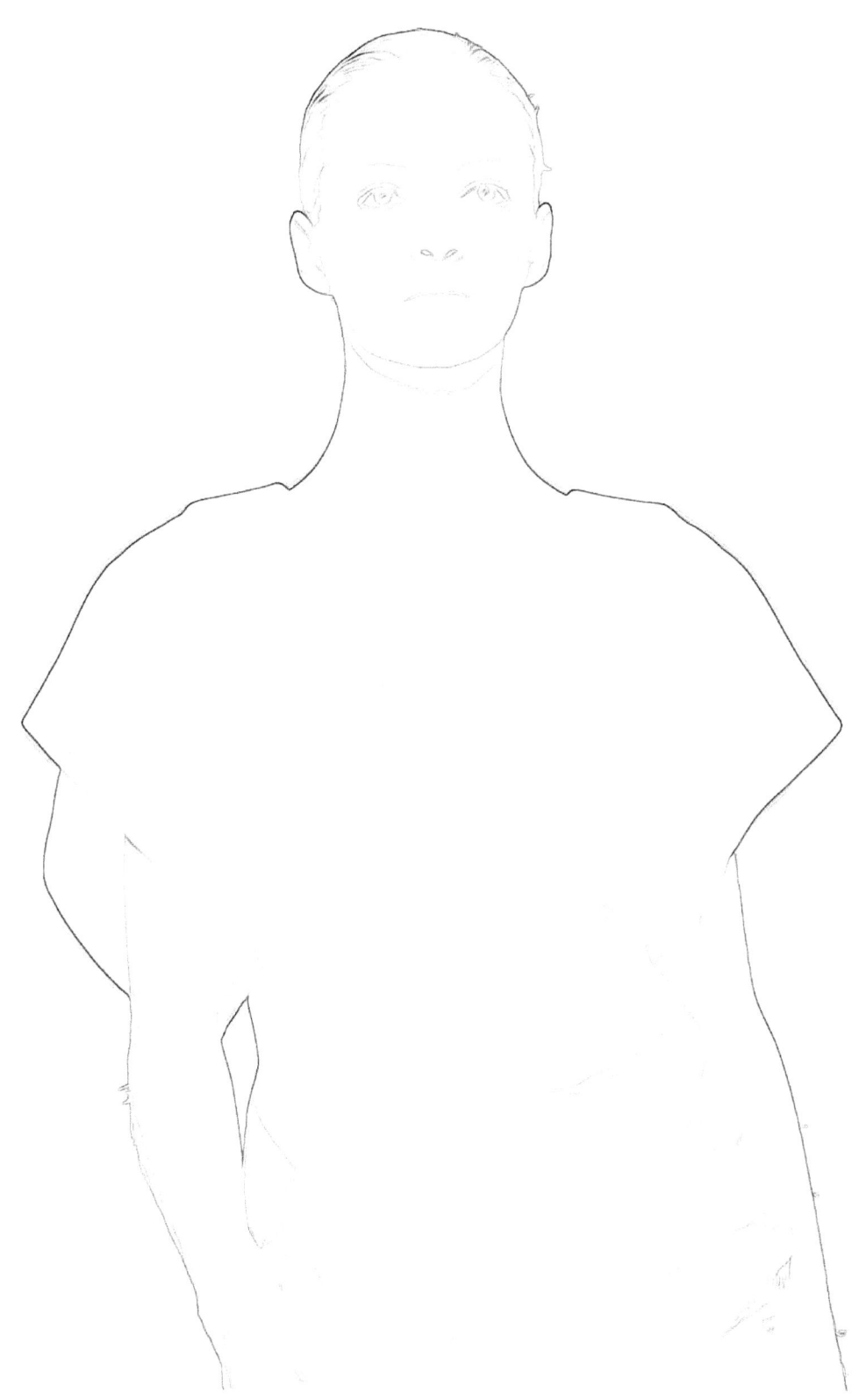

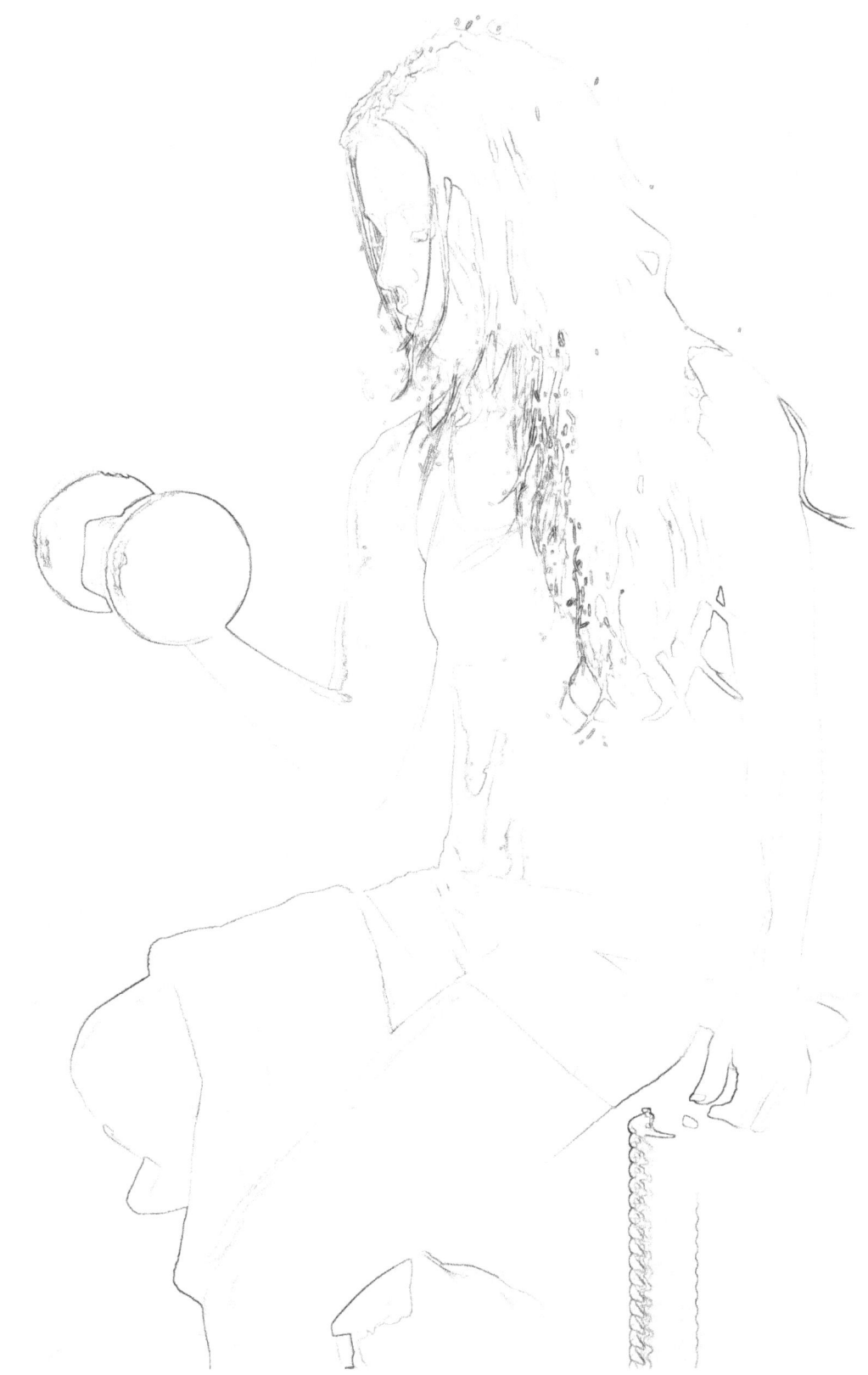

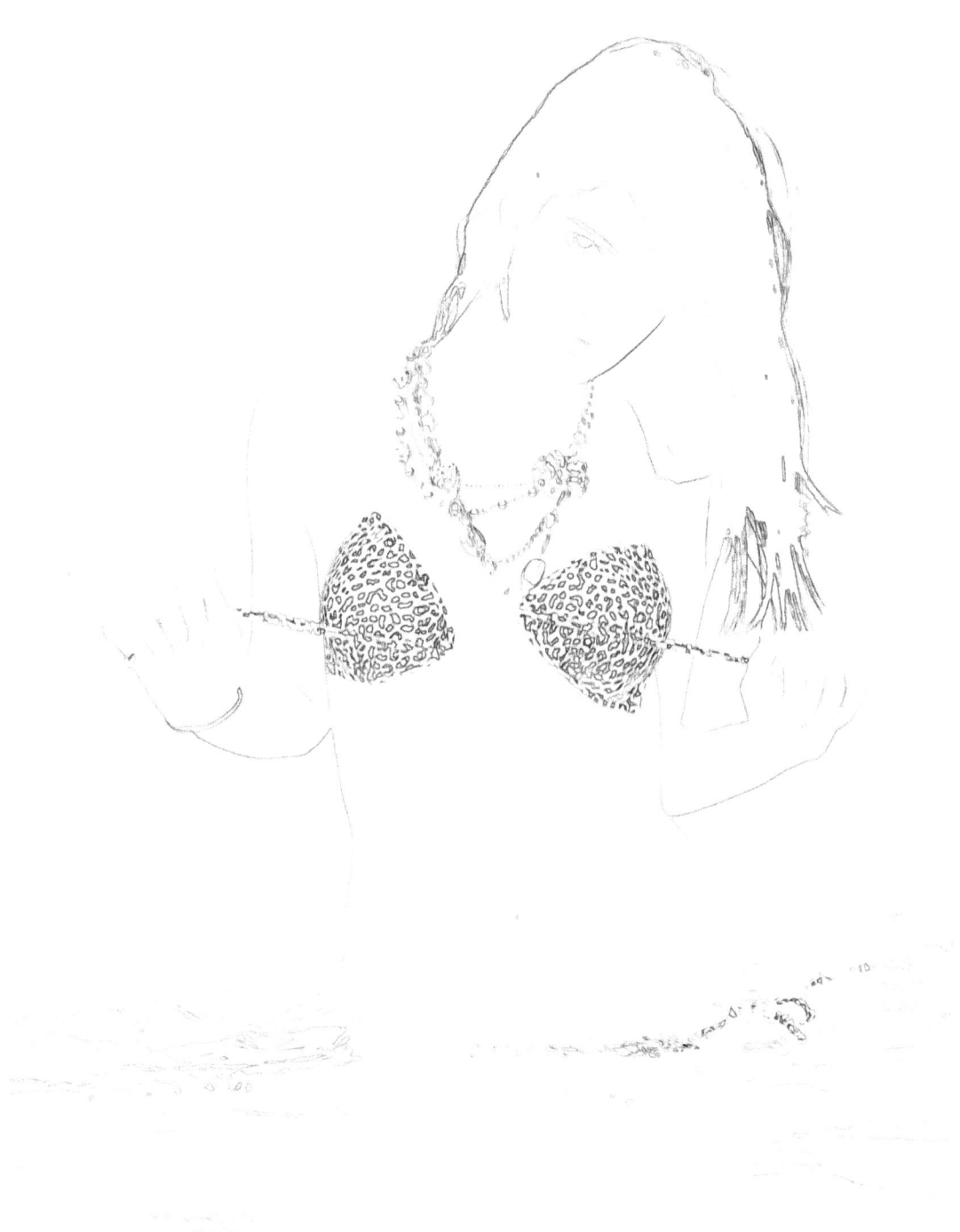

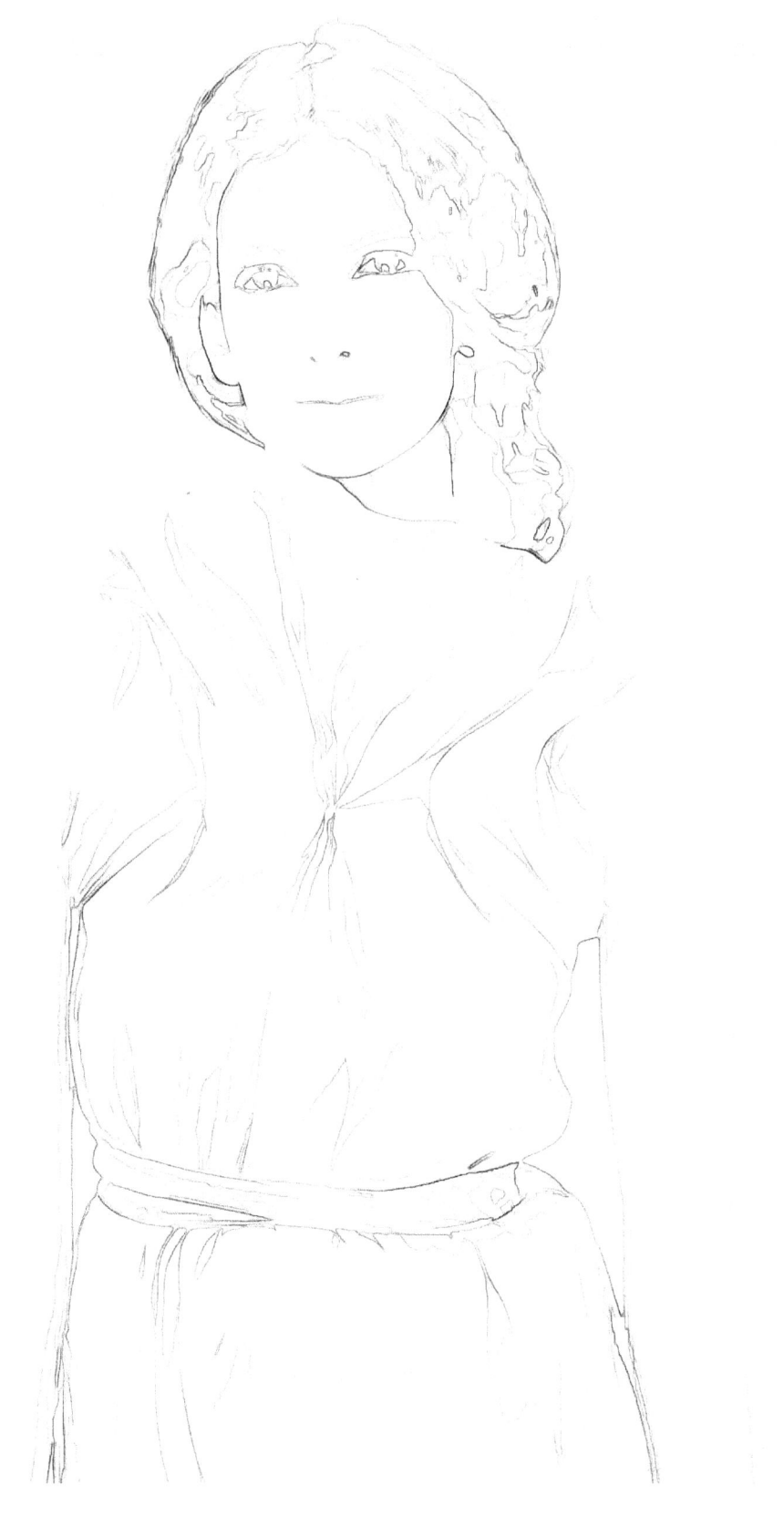

Thank you

PDF Version this book :

http://bit.ly/fashion_2_k

Don't Miss Another our Books.

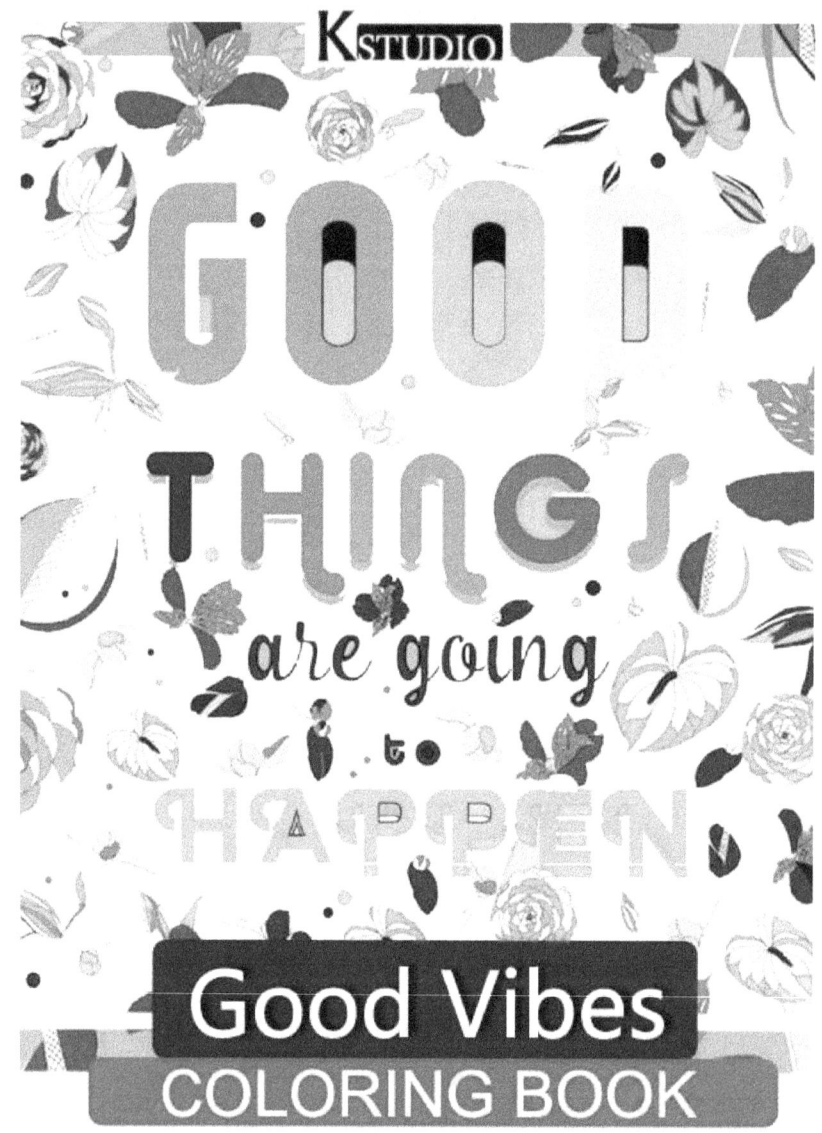

ISBN : 1530381223

www.ingramcontent.com/pod-product-compliance
Lightning Source LLC
Chambersburg PA
CBHW080551190526
45169CB00007B/2733